Shut the Hell Up:

Let the Heaven Do Some Talking

By

Ryan Krempels

Where's your strength in your darkest hour?

It was December of 2012. The house was quiet. I was one month removed from being officially divorced and due to some tough circumstances, we still lived in the same house together. While we got along well due to a commitment we made to respect and care for one another, tonight, she was not home. She had returned home to Canada for a few days to spend time with her family. Thus, I'm home alone, left to my thoughts and what would turn out to be a near fatal attack from the enemy.

On this night, I was in my room working out. I still remember, nearly 7 years later, I was using a barbell with some weights. Just doing my thing, my favorite thing in fact, when it begins. I begin to think about the poor job I've done as a husband. Unfaithful. Porn addict. Selfish. Not as loving as I could or should have been. I feel broken. I begin crying so hard, just so slammed with this reality that I have fallen so short of what God called me to. I stop lifting, go to the bathroom, finish crying, dry my tears, wipe my face and go back to my room. A few minutes later, the same thing happens. So, I cry it out again, go clean up, back to working out. This pattern continues for the next hour. Yes, an entire hour. Over time, other events from life came to mind, almost like the devil was working to remind me of other moments in life where I was awful. Isn't that just how the devil works sometimes too? Sees an opening and brings the cavalry? As the hour goes on, I begin to think maybe it's better if I'm not around anymore. I begin to get nudged towards this idea that ending my life is the best thing for everyone.

Taking my jump rope, I somehow figure out how to tie it to my coat rack and form a noose (to this day, I'm not sure how that happened). Now I'm standing there, contemplating this decision when all of a sudden from the depth of my soul rises these words: "Nothing in all of creation can ever separate me from the love of Jesus Christ." I say them out loud. I say them again. I don't remember how many times I said that but it was a few and each time with more oomph and conviction. Then I have the great revelation. If NOTHING can separate me from God's love, then I have a choice right now since I'm still breathing and that means I'm still loved. I can A) do this, thinking it's for the best and then bring pain to my parents and the rest of my family as well as suffering other consequences like missing out on God's plans for me (plus, on a lighter note, it would mean no more Starbucks or NFL Sundays, I'd never see Europe and 100 other things I'd never get to experience) on top of the fact that taking my life is basically an admission that I don't believe God can make good from this or B) press into God like I've never pressed into Him before and either get my miracle or die trying (no pun intended).

Robert Frost once penned these words.

"2 roads diverged in a wood and I took the one less traveled and it has made all the difference. "

Amen to that. And that's where our story begins. This book on the power of right words being spoken over us is the culmination of the past 7 years of God moving in my life. It is largely the stories and the lessons I've learned over this time. Granted, I haven't, and can't, include every sermon I've listened to and how it enriched me, every story and what's it's taught me, every trial and how I grew from it, every blessing and how it help me feel close to God and see the Father's heart, each person who has come and gone that God used to impact me in one way or another.

These lessons on the power of speaking faith-filled words are one of the most transformational things that I've been blessed with these past years. My hope and prayer is that just as God has used others to open my eyes in this area, God will work through this book and help you as well so that you may go forth equipped to speak life over your life and be properly equipped for your own journey.

What's up with this?

I am aware that there may be atheists, agnostics, skeptics, those who have left the faith, even some Christians or others, who have very strong opinions on this idea of a positive confession. I respect their beliefs and I'm not interested to get into an argument with anyone. I do realize as well that some preachers, labeled "prosperity preachers" really do seem to take an approach that we can/should prosper as Christians. I'd like to be perfectly clear about where I'm coming from with this though. I DO NOT believe that I, as a Bible-believing Christian, can have anything I want. If that was the case, believe me, I'd have been confessing "Katy Perry wants to date me" years ago (don't judge me. She grew up in a Christian home and her dad's a pastor. Maybe I'm the one to bring her back to faith. Lol). Or for sure I'd be saying "I own an Acura TLX," my dream car. No, though. That's not how this works at all. Here's what I DO believe - I believe that I can have anything the Bible says that I can have. Period. The Bible may not say I can have houses or cars or a big bank account just because I speak it into existence but it does say I can have joy, peace, purity, freedom and so much more. I'm not talking about prosperity in the world, only prosperity in the spirit. To my beloved reader, this book has been and is just for you, though, and here's how you can be proactive to have everything the Bible said YOU can have and find transformation for every area of your life.

Are you serious about pursuing life change?

I'm not sure if we need another book on the power of our words. However, this book isn't intended for every single person. It's only meant for people who speak words. Is that you? As a side note, I apologize for anyone who has any sort of limitation in regards to speech. I certainly do not mean to offend but the aim of the book is to enlighten us to what words come out of our mouths. So, this is indeed geared for those of us with the disposition to speak words that hinder. If you are a person who speaks words, then it's likely that there is at least some nugget of information in here that's going to benefit you. Maybe you've already learned much on the topic of the power of words. That's fantastic! Are you applying it? Maybe you know very little or nothing. Maybe you're naturally positive and words are already manifesting themselves in a positive direction. Then maybe this book just helps equip you with knowledge about principles you're already living out. Whatever the case may be, whether you need help in this area or just some regular maintenance, I believe this could be a helpful resource for you.

My ultimate hope isn't to help thousands of people, truth be told. The world is too big and that's far too much pressure. I've been thinking about this idea lately, asking myself how can I get this published, how can I get this out to people all across the United States and beyond, how can I find and reach those who could most benefit from this sort of information and what I hope would be an ensuing revelation. Wow!! How is one person supposed to do that? That's way too much for this one guy from a small town in Pennsylvania. So, I've set a different goal that isn't overwhelming and would be so incredibly heart- warming to see accomplished. My goal that I'm setting for myself right here on Day 1 of writing this manuscript is to impact one person. That's it. Nothing too lofty. No pressure. If one single person can read this, get it, begin to be conscious of words they speak and realize they have what it takes to not only change their life but also to change the trajectory of it, then my efforts to write all this down and share it will have been justified.

Maybe you're a person who just can't move past a struggle with your particular vice or you have anger issues or you complain a lot or you can't get that one experience off your mind and it's like poison. Then this is for you and can help you. Just as I had different resources –

sermons, books, videos, etc – that equipped me, I now come to equip you so you can take a step towards that long sought-after goal of victory in your life.

I want to make you some promises, reader. I promise that everything in here (minus the stories from someone else) is something I have personally experienced. This book isn't the result of me asking "Hmm, what's something popular I can write about that people would benefit from learning more about?" This book is personal to me. This book is MY journey from naive to enlightened. Everything in these pages is the bona fide truth of my experiences over the past few years.

I also promise that I will do no research whatsoever for this book (Confession. I wrote this only to later look up how many books in Psalms David wrote himself. Homer Simpson moment. Doh!). I'd hate for someone to think that I'm an author and I spend hours researching this topic, educating myself about various things. Ummm…..whatever. You're gonna get the authentic, Ryan. No more, no less. All that you're about to read is straight from my brain to yours. The only exception to the researching thing are the Bible references.

The last promise I want to make to you is to be real and genuine. I want you to read this and feel like you and I are sitting on the couch in my living room or we're at a café or hanging out on Facebook messenger together. I'm thinking about you as I write this because I'm writing it TO you. I'm more interested in making this feel personal than I am in sounding professional or like a polished writer or anything like that because I'm absolutely not that. I'm just a regular guy who worked back office at a bank for a few years and was able to load up my mp3 player with sermons and listen to those all day. Consequently, I learned a lot of stuff and having seen how it's transformed me, I want to pass along the knowledge. Cool? Aaaannndddd……now you see what I mean. Hahaha. At least for me and what I want to address here, I think you and I will connect more with a personal approach than if I just sit here and talk at you and tell you what you should be doing. I'd like to call this a café writing style (did I seriously just coin that phrase? Go ahead, say that out loud. Did you do it? Sweet!! You owe me $10 for royalties). I already know this stuff and I care and I want you to know it. Let's hang out together.

I do feel the need to preface a warning though. Don't think for a second that you're going to read this and "get it." I hear you, Ryan. Boom….problems all gone. No, it's going to take work. What took time to get yourself into is going to take even longer to get out of. But it's possible and you have what it takes. These principles are going to show you how to harness the ability you already have in a way that will

16

help you to move you in the direction you desire to go.

It's also going to take commitment. I can guarantee you the devil doesn't want you reading this. He's not going to just roll over and let go. You're going to have to fight for what Jesus died on the cross for you to have and the devil can't do a darn thing to stop a person who has set their mind towards victory. So, this is going to take commitment.

So, are you the person that this book is for? Are you the one person who's tried so many other things but this particular approach is the answer you've been looking for? Then let's get rolling. Perhaps you've heard the Chinese proverb "The journey of a thousand miles begins with a single step" before. Maybe this is step 1. Maybe it's step 273. Either way, thanks for allowing me to help you take one more. And reader, congratulations on your inevitable victory.

How do your words steer you?

We talk a lot. I know I talk a lot. Right now, my family is offering up a Southern amen. You know, that's where you lift one hand, pat the air while saying "amen child." Yes, I talk a lot. Whether we speak a lot of words each day or very few, it's not the quantity of those words but the quality.

In James 3:2-10, James writes about the power of our tongues. He points out how a ship's rudder can steer the direction of a ship, how the bridle can steer the direction of a horse, how a small spark can set a forest on fire and how if we could control this small thing, we could control ourselves in every other way also. So, what is the quality of your words and are they steering you in the direction that you want to go? Proverbs 18:21 says *"The tongue has the power of life and death."* Are you speaking words of life or words of death, ones that lift up or ones that pull down?

It's only about 9 or 10 years ago that I began to learn about these things. I was 30 or 31. Certainly not some teenager who gets his life together by getting his mouth to speak the right sort of life-giving words. I spent many years speaking unhealthy words before I began to learn how powerful those words are and how to change them so that my life could begin to change. Oh, how thankful I am now for what I've learned and the work I put in but I'm sad knowing many are where I used to be, unaware of the potential that lies before them to change those parts of themselves that they want to change and in a certain sense, it's so easy.

I remember a girl I met at church a few years ago. She was very cute and had a nice smile. I went home from church one day to discover a message from her waiting for me on Facebook. Oh snap, somebody's checking out my action and liking what she's seeing. Yes! So, we begin talking and it's a good time. However, one day, as we're talking, she makes the comment "I'm not attractive." Excuse, me but you're not? Because that's not exactly the criteria I would list on an online dating profile that I'm looking for in a potential dating partner, sorry to admit. As we continue our conversations, she makes this same sort of statement other times. During other chats, she would say "I'm never going to meet anyone." So, what are we doing here then?? As she says these sorts of things, unknowingly, she begins to affect the level of my romantic interest towards her. The fact that we didn't have much in common is a whole other issue and not really the point I am working to make. That she would

declare her level of attractiveness to me
(can I make my own determination?) shows
the power of our words to impact not only
ourselves but potentially the view that
others would have towards us as well.

How close is your answer to prayer?

Let me ask you a question. What if the healing you've been praying so fervently for is planned to arrive tomorrow? It's understandable if your reaction right now would be similar to what mine would be if someone asked me a question like that. "That would be awesome but how would I know that's what is going to happen?" And the answer is that we wouldn't know. What if God's on the verge of giving you a revelation about that struggle can't shake? Maybe, just maybe, in regards to healing, God's just about to bring some healing but you've been speaking over yourself "I'll never be healed." Perhaps God's response then is something along the lines of "Oh, you won't? I was just about to heal you but if you say you never will be, then okay." Hey, I don't know if this is how God is or how things work but I do know we should have faith and let that be evident in our words. As a side note, if you're a believer (an active tense word as opposed to a believed, someone who did actively believe but hit a hard time and now doesn't), then you believe you're going to Heaven and you probably believe the Word and verses like Romans 8:23 *"And we believers also groan, even though we have the Holy Spirit within us as a foretaste of future glory, for we long for our bodies to be released from sin. We, too, wait with eager hope for the day when God will give us our full rights as his adopted children, including the new bodies he has promised us."* So, you see? It's strange to confess that you won't be healed when, as the Bible is clearly telling us, healing is our destiny.

Maybe, just maybe, God's about to make your path cross with that special guy/girl you've been hoping and praying to meet but you've been saying things like "I'll never meet anyone. I'll always be single and alone." Not exactly a motivator for God to open that door, don't you think? What if a desperately needed revelation about yourself is nearly yours but you've been complaining or speaking about how nothing will ever change or truthfully, speaking anything except faith-filled words? What if your dream job is around the corner tomorrow? My friend, I don't know any of this. I'm only trying to throw out some questions for you to consider. Bottom line is, we need to have faith. Hebrews 11:1 says *"Faith is the confidence that what we hope for will actually happen; it gives us assurance about things we cannot see."* What if what you want is right there but because you aren't God, you are unaware of its proximity. I'd like to tell you a story about an experience that Louie Giglio had once on a trip.

Louie was booked for a speaking engagement away from home. So, he flies there and is kindly picked up at the airport. On the way to his hotel, he's chatting with the person driving him and this guy is starting to make a big deal about this room that was booked for Louie. "We hope you enjoy your room," "Wait until you see this," those sorts of things. He arrives at the hotel and gets a bit of the same treatment there in regards to his room. They take him upstairs to get settled. Well, all the fanfare didn't exactly match up with what he actually saw. He was quite unimpressed by his surroundings but of course you're not going to actually say that to your hosts, let alone ones who seem to be so excited about what they're gifting you. As he tells it, it was more like an overgrown closet or something. Just not very big. A bit later, he goes to the event that he's there to speak at. The organizer or someone "in the know" gives him a funny smile, asking him how he likes his room. More of this? That evening when he's back at this room hanging out, he decided to order some room service. The food arrives and he hears a knocking but it's not actually at his door. He gets up and peeks outside only to discover the guy at the door next to his. The guy comes over to where he's at. Now, I'd love to remember this story 100% but I don't. Pardon me from having only heard it once and that being like 7 years ago. What I do remember is the guy found it odd Louie was where he was but then realized Louie was unaware. So, the guy comes into the closet a.k.a the room, walks over to a set of doors and opens them up to the most ridonculous (if you don't know what that slang word means, ask a fellow human who's a bit less "life seasoned") room. It would seem that Louie had gone into the wrong door and was actually in a small side area of his REAL room, not the monstrosity that was actually gifted to him. Can you even imagine how wide his eyes must have been? Can you imagine how exciting that would be or heartwarming, knowing how amazing of a gift awaited you and that someone had set apart specifically for you out of love and gratitude?

Now my friend, I ask you – what if, and I'm not God so I absolutely don't know but just want to ask you a question to get the cogs in your brain considering this, what if your "next door room" is RIGHT THERE......but you keep complaining about your current spot or maybe you act like Abraham's father, Terah, in Genesis 11:31. *"One day Terah took his son Abram, his daughter-in-law Sarah and his grandson Lot and moved away from Ur of the Chaldeans. He was headed for the land of Canaan but they stopped at Haran and settled there."* Have you settled for your little closet, my friend?? Maybe you've complained. Maybe you've settled. Maybe you just stop believing Philippians 1:6 – "He who began a good work in you will carry it on to completion." You have to look inside yourself and draw your own conclusion. Perhaps you've not heard or don't believe Psalms 146:6 – "He keeps every promise forever." I don't have an exact answer for you.....but I do know who God is and I know absolutely for sure that he's got a "next door room" for you. He's got one for me too. I'm believing for it but if I use my words to speak "I'm never going to have a better job" or "I'm never going to get out of debt," then how can God use me? I'm being closed off. I'm not a believer, just a believed.

I debated about sharing this but I think it's important for me to be transparent with you and while I may feel slightly silly being so open about it, I want you to know that this whole "next door room" thing is absolutely relevant for me. I'm not just writing this stuff; I'm living it out. Right here on this very night of October 10, 2019 in addition to many nights preceding this one, I have a desire to meet someone. I had a very special someone earlier this summer, my best friend ever actually (yes, same girl that you'll hear a bit more about later) and we connected in a way that was like nothing I've ever felt or experienced before. I'm ready to feel that for good. I miss that wonderful feeling of connection. I would really like to meet someone who would say "Ryan, I've been waiting for you. I've been trusting God would bring you and I together at the right time." For me, this is something I dream of. Some people dream of cruises or vacations or meeting a band. Those are true for me too but this area of meeting someone is a dream for me. Here's the thing though – I have absolutely nothing going on in even the smallest way that I could look at and be encouraged by in this area. But I refuse to say "I just don't know if I'm ever going to meet someone." You will not catch me saying "I'm not good enough for someone." What I do tell myself is that I'm worth the wait and even as I say that, my eyes are almost getting watery. I remind myself that

God is in control and 100% of my hope is in him for this area. If the devil thinks that a lack of anything tangible is going to get me doubting, then he's got another thing coming.

My beloved reader, YOU have a "next door room" and it's right there!!!!! Oh, our God is so mighty and I know he wants you to have it just as he wants me to have it. In fact, the Bible says in Isaiah 30:18 (NIV) "The Lord longs to be gracious to you." I am believing by faith for my "next door room" in multiple areas. Will you join me?

What's your attitude towards trials?

I'd like to spend some time talking specifically about trials. I want to dig into that because when we get blessed in a good way that makes us smile, we don't have any problem speaking uplifting, happy, positive words, do we? But when things go south, so does our level of positivity and our quantity of faith-filled words, right? Generally speaking, of course. I'm sure there are people for whom a trial is a bump in the road, not a road block and they stay positive. But for me and perhaps you as well, reader, it's going to be a learned thing. So, lets chat about trials and how they can be an absolute awesome crucible for learning to speak faith-filled words if we allow them to be.

I know that perhaps you'd rather we discuss how we change our words and how that leads to being blessed. In fact, that is what we're going to be doing. Maybe to your surprise, trials can be such a period of experiencing God and growing in Him, which is to say then, blessedness. I'm not going to lie and say that I love trials. "God, that doesn't feel good at all!! Wooo wee! Yeah, bring on hard things." I won't act holier than thou and say I always go through trials with the perfect attitude or that I never complain. However, I am going to tell you how I have learned to rejoice in trials. I want to try to help you take a different perspective in trials.

Why don't we rejoice in trials? Do we lack the physically ability to do so? Like somehow trials just cause us to clam up the positivity and only be pessimistic? Is someone preventing us from doing so? I put that question out on Facebook to see what insights people could offer regarding this. It was pretty neat to get a few people responding and getting some different takes on this.

One response was that we are used to instant gratification. Boy if that isn't true. I immediately picture a child throwing a temper tantrum because the child wants a chocolate chip cookie that the parent isn't too keen on giving and then the parent caves. No judgment on parenting, especially since I'm not one (though, I'M like a big kid and for a few years I've lived on my own. So.....one could argue I'm a single parent. Just saying. lol). We like instant. Doesn't that feel better than God making us wait, even though this process of waiting is perhaps a time of his cultivating in us and testing our trust and faith and preparing things for us? The Bible says in Lamentations 3:25 – *"The Lord is good to those who depend on him, to those who search for him."* Other translations use the word wait rather than depend. I would say that chocolate chip cookie dough batter is delicious but also say that waiting for it to bake and enjoying a soft baked cookie is even better. Can I get an amen? I'd say the anticipation (the waiting for) of a first date is pretty exciting and worth it (unless he, for the ladies of course, takes you to a fast food joint and, being the gentleman that he is, says "You can totally super-size it if you want to." Um....maybe not worth the wait). Sometimes, instant gratification isn't as good as the sought-for blessing afterwards.

I also had someone say that trials cause us physical pain and we can't see the outcome, not one hour let alone days, weeks and months. How true that is! Surely, it's not just me that has heard, maybe even said, "I just can't see how this is going to turn out." Isn't that exactly what faith is though? Or what it means to have faith? I think of the story of Lazarus in John 11. The sisters Mary and Martha sent a message to Jesus that their brother is sick and how does Jesus respond except to wait 2 whole days before going to Judea to see this family. By then he's dead. As you surely know, he raised Lazarus from the dead and glorified God. I kinda doubt Mary and Martha, upon hearing Jesus was going to wait, said "Oh, I see what's going on here." Worked out in the end not too shabby, am I right? Sometimes the wait is a long period. Heck, Jacob had to work and wait 14 years for Rachel. I'd say he thought it was worth the wait. The Bible even says that the time flew by for him knowing he was getting her as his bride. Sometimes we must wait and we don't know the timeline but the outcome just proves that indeed God's ways are higher than our ways.

Another person said we like having things our way. This makes me think of the story of King Saul or even of

Abraham/Hagar/Ishmael. In 1 Samuel 8:5, the elders of Israel went to the prophet Samuel and requested *"a king to judge us like all the other nations have."* God wanted to be their king but they felt that wasn't enough. I guess Chris Tomlin's song "Your Grace Is Enough" wasn't on their Pentecost playlist. Samuel passed along their request, God responded with a warning about having a king and they said yeah that's cool bring it. They wanted their own way, insisted on it, God appeased them and it just didn't turn out well for them. Shocker! Abraham, as you perhaps recall, was given a promise of a child. God didn't seem to move fast enough and so he got with his wife's servant, Hagar, and 9 months later, Ishmael was born. Granted, everything worked out great for Abraham but he wanted his own way and pushed to see it happen. We do like our way. I like having things the way I want them....but God's way is better.

This goes right along with another response I received that said that we like comfort. We sure do, don't we? As pastor Matt Chandler has said before "God is not a genie in a bottle and you're definitely not Aladdin." Might be nice sometimes if God was a bit more like that and we could just enjoy comfort and easy living with a God who gives us what we want when we want it but I'm absolutely sure it would be not as fulfilling as the dream would have us believe.

The last response I received regarding why we don't rejoice in trials was because we don't have a Heavenly perspective. If you want an encouraging song regarding this, listen to Jonathan Thulin's song "Architecture." I love this response. What an absolutely awesome stance to take – maintain a Heavenly perspective. Hebrews 12:2 says we should *"fix our eyes on Jesus."* Or even the hymn

"Turn Your Eyes Upon Jesus" gives great encouragement.

Turn your eyes upon Jesus

Look full in his wonderful face

And the things of earth will grow strangely dim

In the light of his glory and grace

If we could see things as God sees them, everything would make much more sense and we could easily trust. But we can only, by faith, work to maintain a heavenly perspective and get into the Word and trust what it says. This person had also said we need to walk in the Spirit and that we need enough trust in the Lord to know he's good. Nahum 1:7 says *"The Lord is good, a strong refuge when trouble comes. He is close to those who trust in him."* The Bible says in Psalm 118:1 *"Give thanks to the Lord, for he is good! His faithful love endures forever."* Also, in Habakkuk 1:13 the Bible says *"But you are pure and cannot stand the sight of evil."* The NIV has this verse as *"Your eyes are too pure to look on evil."* So, we serve a good God and if we can fix our eyes on him, even to the point of being stubborn about clinging to that as truth, we will maintain a perspective higher than merely being driven by the things we see with our physical eyes.

Though we've been diving into the responses to trials and our thoughts about them, this does still relate to the words we speak. When trials come, the temptation to let the quality of our words sink increases significantly. So, it's definitely important to dig into the roots of trials, see why we respond the way we do and then try to make an alteration to that response. Perhaps we just need to look at them a different way. Not just maintain a Heavenly perspective but actually look at them through a different lens.

A few hundred years ago, there was a famous artist named Michelangelo. Sistine Chapel. Statue of David. Inspiration for future mutant ninja turtle name. Yeah, him. He had an incredible quote that has greatly impacted me and helped me as I go through trials and quite frankly, it's impacted my words, specifically the words I use when I'm praying. He said:

> *"When I look at a block of marble, I see the finished work in it and when I begin to work on it, I merely work to cut away everything that should not be."*

So, I want to ask you some questions. Now, I could just point a finger and say you should trust God in trials or could ask why your faith may falter in trials but I'd prefer to throw out a few questions. After you read them, perhaps you want to sit down with this book and ask yourself these questions or maybe pray over them.

Is it possible, not saying it's a certainty, but is there even a slight chance that as you go through whatever trial you're encountering, its God's grace coming upon you and working to cut away things that should not be? Is it possible he's allowing certain things in order to cultivate deeper levels of trust and faith and seeing his Word come to life? Is it slightly possible he wants you to know his heart more and this is the best way to do it? If your house burned down or you've lost a loved one, to name a couple of examples, then I would say that's likely not God working to challenge/change you. Those are not the sort of things we're talking about. But maybe you've lost a job. Maybe it's an unexpected bill. Maybe your daughter came home with a nose ring, a new tattoo and a boy that you really want to violently lay hands on in prayer. Do you think growing in faith is supposed to be an easy process? Grapes go through a press. Clothes are put under a hot iron. Muscles are strained under barbells with lots of weight on them. Clay sits inside kilns that can be up to 2400°. But what is the result of these intense circumstances? Fine wine. Nicely unwrinkled shirts (Ephesians 5:27 – *He did this to present her to himself as a glorious church without spot or wrinkle….*). Toned muscles that'll make your spouse wanna lay hands on you in prayer. Beautiful pieces of pottery. Now, that's worth the temporary unpleasantness, right? Pastor Jud Wilhite shares a story of a time he endured some unpleasantness.

He went to a YMCA one day. Not a new flashy gym but one of those older gyms where you go down the stairs to it and the lights are old and making that buzzing noise. He's working out and in walks this huge man ready to do some lifting. His name was John. John decides he's going to do some bench pressing and casually asks Jud "Hey, can you give me a spot?" When I heard the podcast in which I heard Jud share this, I'm thinking he must have had a

Robert De Niro-inspired moment. "Are you talking to me?" Jud agrees, though he clearly wasn't sure what help he's gonna give. John lifts the bar, lowers it and begins to knock out some reps. At some point, John hits that moment when he's done, saying "Little help." So, Jud grabs and bar and with all his might, yanks that bar upwards. That sucker didn't move an inch! He tries again offering the only sign he can give that he's really trying, the ever-so-manly grunt. Uuuuggghhh!! Nope, nothing. As he tells it, he begins to think "Oh my gosh, this man is going to die right here in front of me." He's got nothing and just steps back, telling John "Bro, I got nothing." John proceeds to lift one hand while lowering the other, dropping the weights off the end side. The bar then goes flying the opposite direction and John flings the barbell off him. He stands up huffing and turns around to give Jud an unpleased look. Jud confesses in his narration "I'm a dead man." Lol. John goes on to tell him "We're

45

gonna start working out." What do you say to something like that except "Yes sir." So, they begin to work out. That was SO rough. Jud says he was barely able to get his car keys into the door of his car. That night, he's crying out to his wife, "Lori, could you please come brush my teeth?" HAHA. Forward a few weeks later and one day, Jud happens to feel his arms and what do you know, in the midst of something that felt so awful and was so intense, he had been developing some muscle.

In the midst of what you FEEL is so awful, is it possible God is building your spiritual muscle? I can't go into the entire story because it's not all relevant, even if it would provide better context, and it would take way, way too long to share it all but I want to tell you about my summer. I met someone back in February. Instant connection with a completely gorgeous girl who was so funny, so interesting and on top of it, she loved Jesus. After a period of time, she became my best friend and she was the best friend I've ever had. I never felt before what I felt with her. In mid-June, while video chatting, she shared with me that she felt like God spoke to her and told her that I'm not the one for her. Through tears, we chatted and by the time we ended our video chat date (she lived out of the area. No judgement on her delivery method please), she said that would still remain close because of how much we meant to each other. As the days and weeks went by, I tried to stay connected with her but she increasingly seemed like she had some better things to do. She would tell me that she was only trying to enjoy each day but how I felt was brushed aside and not a priority. Then, there was the day when I discovered she posted a picture of her and some other guy, who I later came to realize for sure that she was dating. I'm not ashamed to admit that there were many days that involve tears and not just "I'm cutting onions" type of tears either. Full on crying that comes from a wounded heart.

Through all this, I refused to speak "I'm not good enough for anyone," "Oh, I'll never meet anyone," "God doesn't want me to be with anyone." This time was so hard to work through though! What if I had done this? What if I had done that? It was a tough time but through it all, I kept affirming my trust in God, kept pressing into him and being grateful for his love. My friend, I'm telling you as serious as I possibly say anything, TODAY, I am better for this trial than if I had never gone through it at all. I have such a sense of joy and peace, such excitement for things that I don't even see yet but I'm absolutely believing for because of what I read in the Word. I feel so close to God and feel absolutely changed for the better because of this difficult summer I endured.

Maybe you long to meet that special someone. Is it possible God may need to cut away some things that should not be first? Maybe you want to go to a higher place in your ministry. Maybe God needs to do a little chiseling first. In Matthew 11, John's disciples come to Jesus asking him if he's the one who is to come or should they expect someone else. Jesus flat out tells them to go back to John and report what they've seen and heard. So, my friend, I must ask you – who are you looking for? A God who's going to drop that hot guy/girl on your lap or give you that perfect job or free you from all difficult things or heal you immediately today? Or do you want a God who already calls you his workmanship, who loves you enough that he sent his son to die for you, who loves you as you are but loves you too much to leave you that way, a God who leads you through the valley of the shadow as he cuts away some things while guiding you to a glorious destiny (Ps 73:24)? Are your words in trials ones of gratitude that he's the potter and we're the clay or ones of complaint because God's ways and timing don't match yours? Now is a good time for a story of another trial that I went through. I want you to be reminded that I'm not just writing about this. I've lived this.

Many moons ago in a land far, far away.....okay, this isn't a fairy tale. I'll be serious. It was the best of times, it was the worst of times. Ryan!! For real, haha, I'd like to tell you about one of my most transforming experiences over the past few years.

This starts in September of 2013. I felt like God spoke to me and was directing me to sell my house. No additional info was provided to me. I matter-of-factly said okay, let's do it. It took many months but the following June, I was notified by my realtor that someone was interested. It was agreed the buyer would move in a few weeks later and so the countdown began for me to find a new place. You might expect that since God directed me to sell my house, that once a buyer is found, I'd get the next step in this plan and know where I'm moving to, right? Alex, I'll take "Pssshhhttt please" for $200. Haha. That's a big fat no. Totally not how it happened and wouldn't that just be too reasonable and easy? We know God likes things a bit more interesting sometimes. Stick with me here.

So, I start looking for places to live. I was solely looking on Craigslist because I wasn't sure where else to look and only ads with pictures because I wanted to see what the places actually looked like. I started sending e-mails to prospective landlords. By the time it was all said and done, I must have responded to something like 25 different ads and do you know how many responses I got to those e-mails? 0! The whole time, not one single person wrote back to me to set up a meeting or ask questions or even to inform me that place was taken. How can I find a place if no one will talk to me? On top of it, God directed me to this situation. What's the deal, right?

I chose to have faith in this process though. I was constantly speaking trust and hope over myself. Lord, I trust you. I trust in your unfailing love (Ps 13:5). I have this hope as an anchor for my soul (Heb 6:19). I put my hope in you all day long (Ps 25:5). It's not by might, nor power but by my Spirit says the Lord (Zec 4:6). Blessed is he who trusts the Lord, who makes the Lord his hope and confidence (Jer 17:7). The Lord is my shepherd, I shall not want. He makes me lie down in green pastures, he leads me to still waters (Ps 23:1, 2). Lord, you led me in and I know that you will lead me out. I'm taking an attitude like Shadrach, Meshach and Abednego. I know you can lift me out of this, Lord, but even if you don't, I refuse to bow down to the devil. My friend, in this fallen world, do we need to be equipped with a knowledge of God's Word? You're darn right we do. What if God hadn't given me a love for his Word a few years ago? What sort of words would I have been speaking in the waiting, in that time between when he called me to move and when he moved? We absolutely need to know what's in this book and I'm so grateful for what I know and I'm hungry to keep learning. Back to our story.

So, those were the words, among many, that I was speaking out loud over myself every single day, probably multiple times. Obviously, as time went on, I felt the pressure rising. I mean, this wasn't exactly an option, some decision I made on my own and could unchoose at any moment. I HAD to move! Why won't anyone answer me? I had nights, and I remember this vividly, I'd be in the kitchen cooking and I'd step into the dining room and fall to my knees crying….but fully committed to speaking words of life and even in the midst of those tears, I declared my trust in God's ways, that they are higher than mine.

The day arrived when I found a place that seemed like it would work out but I really wasn't wild about it. It seemed not big enough and it just didn't feel right. In Proverbs 10:22 it says *"The blessings of the Lord make a person rich and he adds no sorrow with it."* I trusted that if this was where I was supposed to go, God would reveal to me why it was the right place, even though I couldn't see it. I went to see the place and agreed to take it. Upon returning home, for some strange reason, I went to Craigslist and looked at places again. Not sure why but I guess I figured I hadn't moved yet and God could still move in this situation. If you remember, I had only looked at ads with photos. Well, I must have forgotten to check that box because all of the ads came up and the 2nd one catches my eye. It was short and sweet and sounded great. For real God?!? Are you moving??

I call the guy and we have a great conversation and set an appointment for a couple of hours later. What's the first thing that you do after something like that? You call your mom and share the news. Coincidentally (or was it?), my mom stayed home from work that day due to being sick and agreed to meet me there and give me a second opinion. We meet this guy and oh my gosh. We get along great! I'll just start listing the perks and you be amazed by what God did. Haha. Because this guy traveled for work, I'd have the house to myself a lot. He was a fellow Pittsburgh Steelers fan. He was okay with me using the 2-car garage for storage since he didn't park there and it would save me renting a storage unit. He was a big sports fan and we had many nights standing in the kitchen chatting about the latest news. He charged me far less than I would have paid in most other places. I didn't need to pay for utilities or internet or cable since he already was. Not enough to prove this was all God? Then let me give you one more. I found a gym that was 5 minutes away that I came to love going to and was such a great blessing. I became friends with a guy I met there and later was able to invite him to church and then see him come to Christ. End of story. How about that whopper?

Let's take a breath. I certainly need one. I'm the one writing but oddly, I feel like I'm rambling. Time for a little pause. Let's enjoy a nice, deep breath. Ah. Relaxed. Okay, think for a second. During ALL that, wouldn't it be reasonable if I had been frustrated at God's seeming lack of care and attention? Would it be understandable if I had complained because God led me in and then it was crickets? Would anyone have blamed me for being mad at God for not moving? Well, call me stubborn but I had just decided to put my foot down and refuse to lose faith. Anyone who's read the Bible knows God does this sort of thing (I wonder if maybe he enjoys it a tad also). What would this have been like if I had less knowledge of the Word and was less committed to aligning my words with that? It should come as no surprise that this experience was incredibly transforming for me in my faith and my life.

In light of how it impacted me, maybe you're wondering "Ryan, since you grew so much through it, would you be okay going through something like that again and growing even more?" Aw hell no!!!! LOL. That was no fun, let me tell you. It's not something I would voluntarily endure again but you know what? Trials and difficult circumstances are inevitable in this life and now I know for sure that I have what it takes to not just survive them, but thrive in them. My reader friend, you have what it takes also. Start speaking faith-filled words now and when the storm comes, refuse to change your tune. The devil won't make it easy. He'll tell you God's forgotten about you and try to get you complaining. He'll try to say God's not going to come through and get you disheartened. Well, you tell the devil the same thing that I like to tell the devil – you can kiss my Bible because I'm pressing on in Jesus' name. So shut the hell up and let your words match God's.

What Bible character
do you relate to?

       We've talked about a lot of stuff so far. Getting your "next door room" and if your words are hindering that. How trials build your faith muscles and can be used for good, even to cut away things that need trimmed. I shared my own experiences of trial and how I tried to endure them with faith-filled words. No matter how many good stories I share with you, though, no matter how many encouraging things I share with you, this whole idea of the power of our words has got to be based on something more solid than pure optimism and good intentions. So, at this point, I'd like to dig into the Bible. Yes, I've shared verses but I want to take a look at the power of our words through the lens of the

Bible. I suppose we could call it the Biblicality of all this. No? You don't like that one? How about Bibleness? Biblicity? Well, anyway, we need to bring the Bible into this discussion. How can we talk about the power of our words and not talk about God's Word? This whole idea must be rooted in this book or else it's nothing more than a good practice for our lives.

The Bible has all sorts of references to this idea not only in instruction but also lessons we can glean from the lives of some pretty big heroes of faith. In fact, sometimes I like to read a chapter in Proverbs that corresponds with the day of the month that it is. Two days before writing this particular section, it was the 10th day of the month and so I read Proverbs 10. Wouldn't you know it…..there were 4 verses referencing our words.

*v11 – the words of the godly are a
life-giving fountain*

*v13 – wise words come from the lips
of people with understanding*

*v20 – the words of the godly are like
sterling silver*

*v32 – the lips of the godly speak
helpful words*

This doesn't even include the 8
other verses that reference talking/advice.
So yes, words are both very important and
very Biblical. We could think back to the
reference from James 3 but instead let's
dive into the lives of some people from the
Bible, people we look up to and who clearly
loved God and let's see what sort of words
they spoke and see what we can learn from
them.

Caleb

Let's start with Caleb. He was an important man. Out of the million or so Israelites, he was selected as one of the twelve to go spy out Canaan (Numbers 13). This land is one that God himself called "the land I am giving to the Israelites." So, twelve men go out for forty days and return with their scouting report. Ten men admit the land is bountiful but point out how powerful the people are and how fortified their towns are. Caleb responds saying "Let's go at once to take the land. We can certainly conquer it." Is that so funny? God says he's giving this land, most of the group becomes scared of going and Caleb's all like "Man, we got this." The people go on to argue with him and Joshua, who joined in advocating taking what God already had for them and then the people eventually wanted to stone these guys. So, Caleb has awesome faith and that's clearly showing through with his words.

I'd like to focus in on a time much later in his life though. Eventually, the Israelites reach the day when they've conquered everyone and the land begins to be divided amongst the various tribes of Israel. Caleb approaches Joshua, who is now leading the Israelites. Caleb reminds Joshua of a promise Moses had made to him, namely that the land he spied out would become his because he had "wholeheartedly followed the Lord" even when his brothers frightened everyone else with their report.

I don't wanna paraphrase this next part because it'll dampen the power of Caleb's words spoken over himself and with regards to what was promised him. This is beautiful. Read Joshua 14:10-12 for yourself.

Now, as you can see, the Lord has kept me alive and well as he promised for all these forty-five years since Moses made this promise – even while Israel wandered in the wilderness. Today I am eighty-five years old. I am as strong now as I was when Moses sent me on that journey and I can still travel and fight as well as I could then. So give me the hill country that the Lord promised me. You will remember that as scouts we found the descendants of Anak living there in great, walled towns. But if the Lord is with me, I will drive them out of the land, just as the Lord said.

Am I the only one with a huge smile? Can you hear the stern declaration of his faith, his confidence, his awareness of the Lord's promises? Isn't that awesome? We need to do that! Psalm 138:2 says that the Lord's promises are "backed by all the honor of your name." Have you ever put your foot down and declared you have what it takes and then told God that you're holding him to his promises?

Mary

Do we even need any back story for the mother of Jesus? We know it already. Virgin. Young. Unknown. Not exactly an A-lister for Jerusalem night clubs. Yet, the Lord sees fit to use her to birth his only begotten son. God sends an angel to give Mary the scoop on what's about to happen. The only question she seems to ask is how it's going to happen that she would give birth to Jesus. You know what her response was? Yes, she agreed, you're correct but do you know what she actually said? Oooh, I'm excited to tell you. Check this out.

I am the Lord's servant. May everything you have said about me come true. (Lk 1:38)

Do you see her speaking identity over herself? "I AM the Lord's servant." Go ahead and give that a shot. Now try it with the authority granted you because you're in Christ. Feels good, right? Keep saying it. See, now you are aligning your words with the Bible and speaking life-giving words. No more "I'm not attractive" or "I'm not skilled" or "I'm a loser." I AM the Lord's servant!!

Isaiah

Isaiah is one of the three major prophets in the Old Testament. We don't learn too much about him beyond that but this one fact in itself should tell us of his importance. Unlike Caleb, with Isaiah we're looking at words spoken over a person that aren't filled with life. Let's go to Isaiah 6:5.

Then I said "It's all over! I am doomed, for I am a sinful man. I have filthy lips and I live among a people with filthy lips. Yet I have seen the King, the Lord of Heaven's armies.

Notice four negative statements in a row, one right after the other.

It's all over

I am doomed

I'm a sinful man

I have filthy lips

I suppose the third one is more of a confession but it also depends on how you're saying it. Isaiah adds an interesting note at the end of this. *"Yet I have seen the*

King, the Lord of Heaven's armies." It's like he's admitting that something doesn't add up. I'm sinful but yet I've seen the Lord also.

Look at what happens next. An angel flies to him, touches his lips with a coal from the altar and then declares his guilt is removed and his sins forgiven (verse 7). So while he doesn't speak words that are going to boost his self-esteem, he is forgiven and even extended an opportunity to be God's ambassador.

God

Let's take a look at God himself. Yes, even God himself gets injected into a discussion about the words we speak.

In Exodus 3, Moses is just hanging out in the wilderness, tending some sheep when suddenly the angel of the Lord shows up. "Yo Mo, how you livin'?" No, I'm just kidding. That's not really what the angel said. But hello burning bush, hello God acknowledging the Israelite plight, hello Moses' call to go before Pharaoh. Moses responds with doubt whether he's the right candidate (which is itself something to take a look at but Moses is in the on-deck circle at the moment) and after God provides reassurance that he'll be with Moses. Of course, Moses wonders what he's supposed to say when asked who sent him. And cue God teaching us positivity in speaking our own identity.

> God replied to Moses, "I AM who I AM. Say this to the people of Israel: I AM has sent me to you."

The Lord of all creation needs nothing else added to that. He is. Period. For us, we complete that phrase with things like beautiful, screwed up, confident, never gonna be good enough, blessed, etc. God needs only two words to summarize his identity – I AM. Thank you for leading by example, Lord.

Moses

Let's keep with these two but flip our focus to Moses and we need to advance only one chapter in Exodus to see how Moses speaks about his own identity.

In chapter 4, God begins to reveal signs of his power to Moses by showing him two different miraculous displays of power. That should be more than sufficient for Moses to feel good about going forth with this mission, right? Instead, what does Moses say?

"Oh Lord, I'm not very good with words. I never have been and I'm not now, even though you have spoken to me." (v10)

This makes me think of Caleb and his story. The Lord said he's giving the land....the scouts go check it out. The Lord tells Moses he's going to deliver the Israelites....he wants Moses to go lead them. The scouts return and Caleb, probably with a little swagger, says "Yep, yep. We're gonna conquer that land and those people," when God has already said it's theirs. Moses hears God's call, sees God display his power and then says "I'm not enough," even though God already stated the outcome and that he'd be with Moses. Two men. Two situations where God says "I need you to be my hands and feet." Two different responses. Is there a situation in your own life that you're taking a Caleb-like stance or a Moses-like stance in? What words are you speaking that don't line up,

71

or maybe do, with what the Bible already says we can have or that God will do?

Shadrach, Meshach, Abednego

We can't have a discussion about the power of the words we speak and not talk about Shadrach, Meshach and Abednego. You read earlier about how I applied their example in my own life. So, you know I'm digging this story big time. Let's break this thing down though. These brothers know how to speak truth and speak it with authority. We definitely need to take a note from them.

So, King Nebuchadnezzar.....um, that's way too long. Seriously, I'm not even trying to write that 10 more times. King Neb decides he's the man and a ninety-foot tall gold statue of him should be built and set up in Babylon. Then he sends notice to everyone to come to the dedication. At this event, it's announced that a bunch of instruments are going to sound off and then everyone should bow to worship King Neb's statue. Don't do it and you'll have a date with the furnace. So, the music plays, the people bow, it's all going swimmingly. Only Shadrach, Meshach and Abednego have refused to bow in worship, a fact made known when a bunch of astrologers acted like a group of nine year olds and went to the teacher....King Neb, in this case....to tattle tale.

Of course, he's not having any of that. No sir. He completely loses it and orders them front and center. He gives it to them straight – you have one more chance and if you don't bow, you better find yourself some SPF 20,000 because it's into the furnace for you. In such a beautiful, marvelous, admirable display of faith, courage and trust, look at how these guys respond to this ultimatum (Dan. 3:16-18)

> *O Nebuchadnezzar, we do not need to defend ourselves before you. If we are thrown into the blazing furnace, the God whom we serve is able to save us. He will rescue us from your power, Your majesty. But even if he doesn't, we want to make it clear to you, Your Majesty, that we will never serve your gods or worship the gold statue you have set up.*

Cue more anger from Neb....cue furnace being turned up....cue guys being thrown in only to survive. But their words....look how they just put their foot down. Doesn't it just make you want to do a fist pump? You probably already did like myself. Their response is awesome. In fact, it totally makes me think of the greatest scene from the movie Gladiator. The hero, Maximus, comes face to face with his enemy, the emperor of Rome and with complete disdain he says

My name is Maximus Decimus Meridius, commander of the armies of the north, general of the Felix regions, loyal servant to the true emperor, Marcus Aurelius. Father to a murdered son, husband to a murdered wife and I will have my vengeance in this life or the next.

I literally just went to YouTube to watch that part and despite having seen it so many times, when Maximus says that.......well I can't really share with you how I reacted. Lol. But it made me laugh out loud at myself. Don't we feel that same way about Shadrach, Meshach and Abednego? To have that level of faith where you put your foot down so resolutely is awesome and so inspiring. We have what it takes to do that? Absolutely! You have the ability to align your words with God's Word and speak life. The Bible confirms this in 1 John 4:4. So, you have what it takes. Like a pregnant woman who decides she's in need of a donut and makes her husband go get one (You did this to me!! She may argue to him), you're going to need to set your mind. Speak life because you can. Speak truth because that honors God. Put your foot down today and choose life.

Mephibosheth

Unlike in the previous example where I provided the convenience of a nickname, for this next character, you can just go ahead and pronounce it every time. Haha. We're going to be talking about a guy named Mephibosheth. Yes, Mephibosheth.

Gosh, try saying that 5 times fast. So, Mephibosheth's story takes us back to II Samuel chapter 9.

One day, King David had decided that he wanted to show kindness to someone in Saul's family for the sake of Jonathan. To provide a little background, David had made a promise to care for Jonathan's family should anything happen to him (I Samuel 20). So, upon requesting to know if anyone in Saul's family was still alive that he could show God's kindness to, one of Saul's former servants informed David that Jonathan's son, Mephibosheth, was. David then sent for him.

Mephibosheth comes before the king and after being greeted, says *"I am the Lord's servant"* (v6). David then comforts him, telling him not to be afraid and informs him that David wants to show kindness because of Jonathan and Mephibosheth will receive not only all of the property that belonged to Saul but as well he will eat at David's table. The king's table!! Note Mephibosheth's response after hearing about how he basically just hit the jackpot.

> *Who is your servant, that you*
> *should show such kindness to a*
> *dead dog like me?* (v8)

Maybe you've quickly put together how odd of a response this is in light of what's just been offered but humor me while I break it down. We have a guy who's crippled in both feet due to a childhood accident. He gets beckoned by the king of Israel, basically the most powerful man in that part of the world. He is informed that he's getting the Israeli version of Malibu beach front property. Additionally, Mephibosheth, as a grandson of King Saul, has a rightful seat at the table with the likes of David, Bathsheba (who was so beautiful the king desired her), Solomon (pretty much the wisest man who ever lived and future king of Israel) and Absalom (who was lauded as the *"most handsome man in all Israel. He was flawless from head to toe"* [14:25]). Pretty lofty company, right? Then we got this crippled guy showing up from a town named Lo-Debar. All that and he says what? *"...a dead dog like me."* He is entitled, as a grandson to the former king of Israel, to this incredible inheritance and yet his words to describe himself are anything but grand.

Can you relate to this at all, my friend? Is there a disconnect in your life between what you claim as your identity and what God says is your identity and that you are entitled to? It doesn't matter if you are vertically challenged, got a little muffin top, have the lowest IQ in your family, are socially awkward or anything else. It doesn't matter. YOU are God's workmanship. YOU are entitled to a glorious inheritance. Read Ephesians 1:9-11 and see for yourself. Let your heart rejoice knowing that God has something wonderful in store for you and then let your words be filled with faith and joy.

> *No eye has seen, no ear has heard and no mind has imagined what God has prepared for those who love Him. (1 Cor 2:9)*

David

Ah. David. Shouldn't be too surprising that someone called "a man after God's own heart" is going to close out this section on Biblical examples of speaking faith-filled words. It's not too surprising that a man who wrote 75 of the 150 Psalms would be able to contribute something to a conversation about our words.

David's manner of speaking life, though, isn't like these previous examples where it's been spoken to another person, though Isaiah may be an exception. His is a practice of speaking faith-filled words over himself to himself. Actually, his is the type of behavior that we need to emulate. So, this really is a perfect way to close out our time of looking at people from the Bible.

It was so interesting to comb through Psalms specifically looking for positive confessions that David said over himself. The list is as varied as it is long. Although, I need to confess that I didn't zero in on only Psalms that David wrote. I looked over the book as a whole and since David only wrote half, that means some of what I found was from other authors. How interesting, though, to discover this commonality among the authors of Psalms of positive, faith-filled words. Yes, the list was quite varied but some were repeated many times but that's fine because some declarations are ones that we need to make many times. Anybody ever had a crisis and then declared you're trusting God and then said it a few more times before the day was out? Right. Me too. I'd like to share a portion of the Psalm's declarations that I found. Take note of the variety here. No matter what you're facing or maybe even in what area you wish you were a bit sharper in, aligning what comes out of our mouths with the Bible is all that does matter.

9:1,2 – I will praise; I will tell; I will be filled with joy; I will sing

13:5,6 – I trust; I will rejoice; I will sing

22:22 – I will proclaim; I will praise

27:3 – I will remain confident

30:1 – I will exalt

40:8 – I take joy

42:1,2 – I long for you, O God; I thirst for God

55:16 – I will call

63:1 - I earnestly search

73:25 – I desire you

92:4 – I sing for joy

108:1 – My heart is confident in you, O God

116:14 – I will keep

119 – I will obey (v8)

> *I have hidden (v11)*
>
> *I will delight (v16)*
>
> *I will walk (v45)*
>
> *I honor and love (v48)*
>
> *I meditate (v52)*
>
> *I reflect (v55)*

I believe (v66)

I am determined (v112)

I rejoice (v162)

I obey (v168)

130:6 – I long for the Lord

145:1 – I will exalt

Something that I found very interesting is that between chapters 144 and 150, the word "praise" (or praises) was used 33 times and the phrase "praise Him" was used 16 times. I may not have caught every single occurrence but as I scanned the book of Psalms, the confession "I will trust" was spoken at least 6 times. A confession involving the words worship/sing/thank (or any other worship-related words) was spoken 21 times. It's actually been pretty stinking cool to do this review of Psalms. I, personally, have never noticed this or known this before. It's so neat to see the absolute plethora of positive confessions intertwined throughout this book. What a way to speak!! If you're constantly saying these sorts of things, when would you ever have time for fear or doubt or insecurity? Kinda sheds some light on Joshua 1:8 when it says in the ESV *"The book of the law shall not depart from your mouth."* It's not indicating to avoid talking about the Word. It's instructing us to always keep it in our mouths; don't ever let it depart. Ever tried to talk to a child when they just go on and on and on, even sometimes intentionally because they're trying to annoy you? So, picture you doing that with the Word and then the devil tries to talk to you. Haha. Right? Don't let the book of the law depart from your mouth. Worry and worship can't occupy the same space and if that space is your mouth and you refuse to stop speaking faith-filled words, then worry/doubt/insecurity/etc will get rejected like a Baltimore Ravens fan at a Pittsburgh Steelers tailgate party. You gone!!

So, can we take a cue from David and the other writers of Psalms? Whatever our struggle, let us align our words with God's Word and breathe life into those dry bones of peace or self-control or trust and so on.

Dry bones, Ryan? Oh yes. We should talk about dry bones because we ALL deal with dry bones at times and to look into this, we need to go way back, all the way back to Ezekiel chapter 37.

In Ezekiel 37:1, the Bible says that our title character was carried to a valley filled with dry bones. It seems they were scattered everywhere and were *"completely dried out."* God asks Ezekiel (v3) *"Son of man, can these bones become living people again?"* Ezekiel responds that God alone knows the answer to that question. Check out what God instructed him to do next.

Speak a prophetic message to these bones and say, 'Dry bones, listen to the word of the Lord! This is what the Sovereign Lord says: Look! I am going to put breath into you and make you alive again! I will put flesh and muscles on you and cover you with skin. I will put breath into you and you will come to life. Then you will know that I am the Lord.

Ezekiel obeys the Lord and speaks this message to the dry bones. The Bible uses the word "suddenly" to describe the immediate response to Ezekiel's words. The bones suddenly start rattling, a noise that is carried throughout the valley. It says the bones of each body came together and complete skeletons were then formed. This was all because Ezekiel spoke to those dry bones, speaking words of life. It wasn't just the bones either. The muscles and flesh began to form, then skin covered the bodies. Verse 8 says "*...still had no breath in* *them.*" In verse 9, God instructs Ezekiel again to speak but this time to the winds.

> *Speak a prophetic message to the winds, son of man. Speak a prophetic message and say, 'This is what the Sovereign Lord says: Come, O breath, from the four winds! Breathe into these dead bodies so they may live again.'"*

So, Ezekiel obeys once again and not surprisingly, breath enters the bodies. Every animal *"came to life and stood up on their feet – a great army."* My dear beloved reader, as I put the finishing touches on this story from Scripture and this whole section about the Biblical relation to the words we speak, I want to ask you a question. What dry bones do you have in your life? "Ryan, I was in such good shape in college but now after 3 kids, my body isn't great and I feel unattractive." Dry bones of self-confidence. "Ryan, I've applied for 10 jobs and nobody's reached out." Dry bones of sufficiency. "Ryan, I just can't help it. I get upset. I want to be a calmer person but my temper has a mind of its own." Dry bones of peace and freedom. My friend, EVERYBODY has dry bones but Jesus came so we could....come on, say it with me....have abundant life (John 10:10). These were merely 3 examples but we could discuss 100 more, couldn't we? I'm telling you 100%, you can speak to those dry bones. Acts 17:25 says *"He himself gives life and breath to everything and he satisfies every need."* No matter what your dry bones are, you are meant for more and maybe somebody super cool who's so smart and has 100 friends and is athletically gifted and a calm spirit and so on won't have a right to say that but I have a right to say it because I've dealt with some crap in my life and I've been through the trenches and I'm still standing and I'm better because of it, praise Jesus. I wish I could hug you right now, tell you that you have what it takes and that your dry bones aren't your destiny but I'm going to do something better. Let's close out this whole book by looking at the method of dealing with those dry bones and how we bring them to life.

Give *a man a fish, feed him for a day*

Teach a man to fish, feed him for a lifetime

— — — — — — — — — — —

Where do you want to go from here?

I've been encouraging you as best as I can to speak faith-filled words. I've shared stories to get you thinking about the implications of speaking right words or even the danger of not doing so. I showed you how it's a very Biblical practice and I've stressed the importance of knowing what's in the Word. I have had SUCH a good time sharing all this with you. It's been so fun but I would be remiss if I ended it at this point, getting you all emotionally stirred (maybe, hopefully. Haha) about the words we speak but didn't actually help you to understand HOW we incorporate this as a discipline into our lives. I mean, any fool can get people all excited and convicted. Been to a really good youth conference or Bible teaching seminar

before? Are some churches possibly like
that? You show up on Sunday and the music
is amazing. You just wanna sing and sing
and sing. The message totally hits your
heart and you are pumped up and ready to
go into the world and serve Jesus. However,
later that day watching football with
friends, you're swearing and telling dirty
jokes. You go out to eat and your bill was
mistakenly shorted and rather than have
the integrity to point it out, you figure it's
their loss. You're late for work that week
but the boss didn't notice and so on. I'm not
interested in getting you all jacked up and
full of emotionalism just to send you on
your way and forget everything I've said
and then not be impacted or transformed in
any way. This book is for a person who
speaks words and is serious about using
those words in order to see the trajectory
of their life moving in a positive direction,
seeing positive change in their mind and
heart and consequently, their life. So, you
go grab a shovel cuz we're about to dig in!!

Interesting moment tonight at the gym shortly before I left. Really, I find it so funny and it absolutely proves the necessity for this sort of manual, if you will, on how to change your words to faith-filled. A son, maybe 6 or 7, was encouraging his dad to give the warped wall (a big curved wall you run at, leap and then grab the top and pull yourself up; popular in obstacle course racing) a shot. The dad ran a couple of times but didn't make the jump, ran only. Then he says, get this "I'm too old, I'm too fat to get myself up there."
Ummm.....maybe you don't make it because you're saying you're too old and fat. This proves my point exactly though!! Why would you say that over yourself? Maybe because you don't hear yourself or maybe you think it's trivial. It's absolutely not trivial!! You see, this whole idea of words, putting all the Bible-related aspects of it aside, the foundation of this whole practice of speaking positive words is NOT a Christian issue.....it's a human person issue.

As you surely know, as I illustrated, everybody has this issue. Let's talk about how we change it though!!

Let's start at the spot that was pretty much the spot this got started for me when I was first learning and that's a verse from Psalms and Proverbs. The first is Psalms 45:1 which says *"Beautiful words stir my heart. I will recite a lovely poem about the king for my tongue is like the pen of a skillful poet."* I like how the author writes they will recite a lovely poem, thus declaring the intentionality of their words towards something positive because their tongue, our tongues, are like a pen. The next verse is Proverbs 3:3 and it says *"Let love and faithfulness never leave you; bind them around your neck, write them on the tablet of your heart."* So, you see how these 2 verses come together? Our tongue is like the pen and our heart is like a tablet. Maybe you've never thought of things in that way but I'm sure you've acknowledged it by your actions. Ever had anyone do something to make you feel unattractive and then their words, or maybe lack thereof, found a place on the tablet of your heart and it begins to define you or at least dampen your spirit for a while? Maybe something happened, a lost job or a breakup or a cold shoulder from a potential friend and then you feel like you're not enough and you say that and you then take it on as an identity? We've got to be on guard for what messages we allow to be written on the tablets of our hearts.

At the time of writing this particular section, it's Saturday night, 8:04 pm and I'm home alone. I have 2 female friends, 1 dating someone and 1 two+ hours away, and a few guy friends. I have nobody calling me asking me to get together tonight. I have nobody to call so I can go out this Saturday night and have some fun. Do you know how this affects my value? Not one little bit. Let me tell you what's written on the tablet of my heart and defines my identity after many, many days in the past of speaking faith-filled words.

> *Ephesians 2:10 – I am God's workmanship*

> *Zephaniah 3:17 – He will take delight in you with gladness. With his love, he will calm all your fears. He will rejoice over you with joyful songs.*

> *Philippians 2:20 - I am a citizen of Heaven*

> *Psalm 139 –He knit me together in my mother's womb. I am fearfully and wonderfully made.*

You see, I know who I am and because of that and allowing God's Word to define my value, it prevents everyone else from doing it instead. What are you speaking and consequently writing on the tablet of your heart regarding your identity?

Now that we've laid down the foundation principle in all this, we need to look at the process of getting those right inscriptions put on your tablet. This part is going to take some work on your part. It's really going to take some work but I've been there and I can promise you that the Word works every time. So, fear not, as Jesus has said so many times in the Gospels.

The first step I would say is to find out what area you want to work on. My friend, what's your problem? Haha. For real though, what in your life do you know needs a little tweaking? Don't know who you are in Christ? Trouble with patience? Want a more joyful spirit? Feeling powerless at times in regards to your faith? We should identify the area we want to do some maintenance on and then we'll go to work.

Let's get a little more specific. We'll pretend that I'm the subject here. Let's say that I want to be more hope-filled. Obviously, I need to look up verses that relate to hope. So, I begin to research those and come up with a list of 10. Surely, there are so many more in the Bible but for practical purposes, we only need a portion of those. For me, I usually went with a handful, depending on what I could find and what I like. I'll write those all down and then pick out which ones I like best. That is to say, which ones I can use as self-confessions as well as which ones really resonate with me as I speak them over myself. Let's make up a mock confession list to demonstrate this……or if you struggle with hope and your ears just perked up, maybe this is the start of a list for you. In which case, you're welcome.

So, we found 1 Peter 1:21 that says *"Through Christ you have come to trust in God. And you have placed your faith and hope in God because he raised Christ from the dead and gave him great glory."* That's a keeper! Next, we have the well-known Hebrews 6:19 *"This hope is a strong and trustworthy anchor for our souls."* Then there's Psalm 25:5, *"Lead me by your truth and teach me, for you are the God who saves me. All day long I put my hope in you."* I find Isaiah 40:31 *"Those who hope in the Lord will renew their strength"* and I conclude with Psalms 71:5 *"Oh Lord, you alone are my hope."* My list, as I would write it to speak these verses over myself, would look like this.

> *1 Peter 1:21 – I place my hope and faith in God because he raised Christ from the dead and gave him great glory.*
>
> *Hebrews 6:19 – I have this hope as an anchor for my soul*
>
> *Psalm 25:5 – I put my hope in God all day long*

Isaiah 40:31 – I hope in the Lord and my strength is renewed

Psalm 71:5 – You alone are my hope, O Lord

See how that works? We aren't speaking just any words but we're speaking God's Word as a personal confession over ourselves and onto the tablet of our hearts, resulting in transformation over time. It won't happen after just one or two days of practicing this either. Okay, let's take a look at peace, a pretty common thing people seem to struggle with maintaining. Know anyone who would like greater peace in their lives? Someone who deals with stress or lets things get to them easily? Heck, who doesn't want to be a peaceful person even when the storms of life around you are blowing? Maybe it's something simpler like someone runs a stop sign or red light and you just can't seem to stop letting that steal your peace and you give them half the peace sign. The Bible says we can have peace and so it's ours for the taking. My peace confession list, after the research, would look something like this.

John 14:27 – My peace I leave you, my peace I give you

Philippians 4:7 – His peace, which passes all understanding, will guard my heart and mind

Colossians 3:15 – The peace of Christ rules in my heart

Psalm 34:14 – I seek peace and pursue it

Psalm 119:165 – I love his law and have great peace

You get the gist of it, I think. Does the Bible say you can have it? Then you can have it!! During the 3 years or so that I was actively making/using confession lists, I made 13 of them. Lol. It sounds so crazy now but it's true. 13. As a personal rule, I never worked on more than 3 areas at a time. Thoughts, power, strength, joy, peace, loving the Word, a more worshipful spirit. I didn't want to try to knock it all out in one shot. Rome wasn't built in a day, ya know? God's the potter and some things just simply take time. Notice I said "During the 3 years...?" Don't misunderstand me. I still like to speak the Word but simply, it's just not necessary for me anymore to be speaking peace over myself every day from a confession list. I have it! I don't need to speak about my identity in Christ. As I indicated a bit ago, I know it. I don't need to speak about humility. Man, I'm the most humble person I know. Lol. I rock at humility! You get my point. In fact, just earlier today (on the day I was originally writing the rough draft) I was speaking Ephesians 2:10, Romans 15:13, Nehemiah

8:11, Psalm 73:24 and a few other verses that now escape me. Point is, I still do it and it's great. I don't stop speaking the Word but I don't have some set structure for it. It's just part of me and anytime, I can just speak some peace or joy or worshipful verses over myself. Woo wee....I love it!

One final note about my own personal practice history. Just a little something I want to share that might answer a question for you about what this sort of discipline could look like in your life. What I liked to do was leave my printed-out list on my dresser and do it each morning and then in the evening when I got home from work. Know what happens when you're speaking that out loud twice a day? After a few days, you start to memorize some of the verses. So, then I'm at work, walking to the breakroom doing some confessing (not too loud. Don't want anybody think I'm nuts. Haha. They'd only learn that if they hung out with me. Lol) or maybe when I'm walking to or from my car. Over time, I was probably speaking those lists (in part at least) 6 or 7 times a day, generally sticking to one list for 2-3 months or until whenever I felt like it had satisfied its objective. That'll get engraved on the tablet of your heart, right? And it did and I'm so grateful.

You may feel it's strange to be walking around talking out loud to yourself. If you're a guy reading this, I don't even wanna hear it from you about talking to yourself!! Sunday during football season. Need I say more? Tell me I'm wrong. If you're a woman, well you're flawless and beautiful. I have only compliments for you. But if I was to venture out boldly and suggest something, I might go with that moment you walk into the kitchen after a long day at work and see a sink full of dishes. "Ugh. Why can't he ever clean up when I work late." Mmmmm hmmmm. Right now, just picture me with 1 hand on my hip with that "you and I both know that happens" look. Lol. Close the door to your room, go on a walk, find an isolated place, whatever and take 5 minutes to speak faith-filled words over yourself.

Something really cool that happened in my experience of practicing this was that my radar for positive and negative words was turned on. I became more sensitive, more aware, of the words I spoke but also more easily took notice of other people's as well. Remember my story from just a bit ago about the guy at the gym? Stuck right out to me when I heard it. I can still remember the exact place I was at in my car a few years back when I was driving and in response to something I did that really was rather foolish, I said "Oh man, I'm such an idiot." AS SOON as I said that, as soon as it came out of my mouth, I heard it. Imagine if I had you open your mouth and then I threw dirt in there. Would you say "Hmmm.....there's dirt in my

105

mouth" or would you spit it out? Spit it out of course because it doesn't belong there. As soon as I said that out loud to myself, I responded immediately with "Wait. No, I'm not an idiot. The Bible says that I am God's workmanship. What I did was not smart but I'm not an idiot." See the difference? You can acknowledge something without speaking it over yourself – I am, I have, I always, etc.

As you begin to cultivate a practice of speaking faith-filled words, I believe your radar will be turned on also and then you'll begin to notice those moments when you do not align your mouth with Biblical truth. In turn, perhaps you'll begin to notice these moments in others as well and maybe have opportunities to be an encouragement to them about it. If you're a husband and your wife is having a tough time with something and she's not speaking faith-filled words, because you noticed it, you can encourage her. "Sweetheart, I think you need to shut the hell up" and my friend, I've got a couch that you can crash on for the next month after you give her that loving encouragement. Lol.

Most days, as a general practice, regardless of what areas I was working on, I would speak 1 John 4:4 and Isaiah 54:17 over myself. The one I really loved using often to "cap" off my time of confession is from the ever-popular Isaiah 55 and it's found in verse 11.

The Word does not return to me void but it accomplishes everything it is sent out to do

Amen and amen. Isn't that a beautiful close? We can trust God's Word to do what it is sent out to do. So today, be a believer, not a believed. Be a believer today in God's Word.

In closing, when Nelson Mandela was serving 27 years in prison on Robben Island, he used to recite a poem titled "Invictus," (yes, now you know where the name of the movie starring Morgan Freeman came from). The final 2 lines of that poem are:

I am the master of my fate

I am the captain of my soul

Friend, how are you captaining your soul? Turn the wheel and begin to captain in the direction that you want to go. On the journey from here to there, I am waiting for you there, although that's not to say that I don't have my own growing to do because I do but you know what I'm trying to say. I've got a sweet high five and a giant hug waiting for you. So, go redirect the ship and experience with me the wonderful joy of God's transforming grace and his mighty power. It comes with much lighter living and lots of smiling. It's awesome! Ooooh, I'm so excited for you to get started and to hear your story. This is gonna be so cool. I mean…..*clearing throat* I told you I talk a lot. Lol. Gonna be quiet now so that you can go take back your tongue and life from the devil. Be blessed my brother/sister. Ryan out.

My dear friend, thank you for taking the time to read this and allowing me to share with you. Have you heard any of this before? Many years ago, when I was listening to sermons at work and began hearing about confessing the Word, it was brand new to me. I never heard of such a thing before but I was fascinated by it. I completely saw the logic in it and over time, saw the transformational effect of it. I very much hope you will begin to incorporate this discipline into your life. Yes, I laid out for you how I went about doing it but please know, you are not alone in this. I am here for you. If you need any help to get started speaking right words or you have a certain area you really want to gain the victory in, please feel free to reach out to me at SpeakingtheWord@hotmail.com.

Epilogue

And now to give you 'the rest of the story' (some of our mature readers may recall that line from Paul Harvey)....I have seen many of the situations come to pass that you just read about in Ryan's life. I may not have been there when he was studying the Word and covering his life with the Word, and I certainly didn't know what was happening in December 2012. But I have seen the incredible results of what he has done in his life to become the man that I know him to be today. Let me give it to you straight from the mom's perspective. He was a difficult kid....bad temper, socially awkward, strained family relationships, only ate about 6 different foods, oh did I mention bad temper. Yes, there were several holes in the walls of our house due to that temper. It's probably hard to believe what I'm saying after just reading this book and thinking could this be the same person. Can we say, 'oh but for the grace of God.' It is nothing short of the power of God in someone's life when you see this kind of change. But we do have to reach out for that power and that's exactly what Ryan did on that dreadful night in December 2012! And God has been showing up ever since.

Where once there was a strained relationship between us, today Ryan is not only an amazing son but a great friend. I mentioned those 6 foods he ate back in the day, well today he not only eats healthy foods, but he eats more different cuisines than I do, Syrian, Egyptian, Ethiopian!! And that temper, well, pretty much non-existent. He has such a peaceful and joyful spirit! He always has a word of encouragement for people and his positivity is fun to be around!

I am so happy that Ryan was willing to open himself up to you the reader...the good, the bad and the ugly! It's only when we share what we've been through, that we can impact someone else's life in an encouraging way. I hope you will take his life application of the Word seriously for your own life. And feel free to message him!! He wrote this book for YOU, and nothing will bless him more than to hear that your life has been impacted by him sharing his life with you!!!

Many blessings,

Vicki Krempels

Recommended reading

Your Bible

Honestly, did you think I was going to
suggest Nicholas Sparks or something? ⍰
(that dude sure can write though!)

Made in the USA
Lexington, KY
20 December 2019